9.95

ZOOKEEPERS

CAREERS

William Russell

The Rourke Press, Inc.
Vero Beach, Florida 32964

Edited by Sandra A. Robinson

PHOTO CREDITS
All photos © Lynn M. Stone

ACKNOWLEDGMENTS
The author thanks the Brookfield Zoo of Chicago and its
employees for enthusiastic assistance in the preparation of this
book

Library of Congress Cataloging-in-Publication Data

Russell, William, 1942-
   Zookeepers / by William Russell.
   p. cm. — (Careers)
   Includes index.
   ISBN 1-57103-056-5
   1. Zoo keepers—Juvenile literature. [1. Zoo keepers.
2. Occupations.] I. Title. II. Series: Russell, William, 1942-
Careers.
QL50.5.R87 1994
636.088'9'023—dc20   93-42482
                                                               CIP
                                                               AC

Printed in the USA

TABLE OF CONTENTS

Zookeepers   5
What Zookeepers Do   6
Who Can Be a Zookeeper?   9
Where Zookeepers Work   11
Feeding the Animals   14
Cleaning Up   16
Training Animals   19
The Zookeeper's Helpers   20
Learning to Be a Zookeeper   22
Glossary   23
Index   24

ZOOKEEPERS

Zookeepers are the men and women who take care of zoo animals. Their job is called zookeeping. It is one of the most important and interesting jobs at any zoo.

Zookeepers — also called keepers — are the zoo **employees** who work most closely with the animals on display. Zookeepers help keep the animals comfortable and healthy.

This zookeeper walks through a forest of trunks and tusks as easily as most people walk through a mall

WHAT ZOOKEEPERS DO

Zookeepers perform many jobs. They clean, feed, help and even train animals. Zookeepers may assist **researchers** who study animal behavior.

Zookeepers watch out for the welfare of visitors, too. One day 6-foot-6-inch basketball star Michael Jordan visited Affie, an African elephant at Chicago's Brookfield Zoo. The elephant keeper was 5-foot-2-inch Wendy Schabacker. Thinking Michael might be a bit nervous, she said, "Don't worry, I'll protect you."

Zookeepers keep a watchful eye on animal mothers to make sure they know how to raise their babies

WHO CAN BE A ZOOKEEPER?

People who enjoy animals often want to be zookeepers, but a love for animals is just a beginning. Most zoos require that keepers attend college for at least two years. Some of the keepers' college studies must be about the lives of animals.

Many zookeepers begin as **interns.** Interns are college students who work at a zoo for six to 12 weeks with trained zookeepers.

Learning to be a zookeeper requires education and on-the-job training

WHERE ZOOKEEPERS WORK

Each zookeeper in a large zoo works with a particular group of animals, such as big cats — the tigers and their cousins. Sometimes the keeper works in an animal's **exhibit** area. The zoo's visitors are able to see the entire exhibit area.

A zookeeper also works in "off-exhibit" areas. These are the animal cages and pens that visitors cannot see. Dangerous animals are kept "off exhibit" when keepers clean their exhibits.

A zookeeper works with a special knife to peel hardened skin from the bottom of an elephant's foot

*Zookeepers sometimes have to raise
orphaned zoo babies like this lion-tailed macaque*

*In training for a flight show, a red-tailed hawk
perches on a keeper's gloved hand*

FEEDING THE ANIMALS

One of the zookeeper's jobs is to feed the animals. The zoo's kitchen prepares a special, healthy diet for each animal.

Animals learn to expect the zookeeper's "groceries" at a certain time each day. They look forward to the visit. Zookeepers deliver treats such as hard loaves of bread to elephants and icy **"fishsicles"** to bears.

Keepers feed many animals in off-exhibit areas.

A polar bear at Chicago's Brookfield Zoo claims her meal prize — a fish-filled ice block called a "fishsicle"

CLEANING UP

Zookeepers have a motto about animal exhibits. "If you wouldn't want to live and eat in here," they say, "the animals wouldn't either."

Cleaning animal exhibits is one of the keeper's most important chores. Keepers also clean the animals' fur, feathers, hooves, beaks and skin.

The keepers' biggest cleaning job is the elephant! A keeper even soaps and sponges hard-to-reach places after the elephant lies down.

Soaping even the ear of an elephant is a big job for the keeper

TRAINING ANIMALS

It is not the elephant's idea to take its soapy bath lying down. It is taught, or trained, to lie down at the zookeeper's command.

In some zoos, zookeepers also train animals to show their skills in tests of strength, swimming, hunting, jumping and flying.

Keepers who train animals work with them each day. An animal that obeys a command earns a food treat.

An elephant learns to follow commands at Tampa's Lowry Park Zoo

THE ZOOKEEPER'S HELPERS

Zookeepers work with many other people at the zoo. A new zookeeper works closely with a more experienced keeper.

All zookeepers work with **curators.** Curators are the people in charge of whole groups of animals, such as all the birds, or snakes and lizards.

Zookeepers also work with the kitchen staff.

When an animal is ill, zookeepers contact a **veterinarian,** the zoo's animal doctor.

If the keeper finds a problem with the walrus flipper, she will contact the zoo doctor

LEARNING TO BE A ZOOKEEPER

People can learn many things about animals in schools. Learning to be a zookeeper, however, requires "hands-on" experience. A person truly *learns* zookeeping only by *being* a zookeeper.

Some of the first things senior zookeepers teach new zookeepers are safety and how the zoo works. The beginning zookeeper also quickly learns how to care for the animals' needs.

Glossary

curator (KYU rate er) — a person in charge of the zoo or of several exhibits

employee (em PLOY ee) — a person who works for, or is in the employ of, another

exhibit (ex IHB it) — the place where something, such as an animal, is put on display

fishsicle (FISH sik el) — an ice block loaded with fish

intern (IN tern) — a student hired temporarily to gain on-the-job experience

researcher (REE sir cher) — a person who studies or observes something to find information

veterinarian (vet er in AIR ee an) — a doctor who treats animals

INDEX

animals   5, 6, 9, 11, 14, 16, 19, 20, 22
bears   14
birds   20
Brookfield Zoo   6
college   9
curators   20
elephants   6, 14, 16, 19
exhibits   11, 16
interns   9
Jordan, Michael   6
lizards   20
off-exhibit areas   11, 14
researchers   6
Schabacker, Wendy   6
snakes   20
veterinarian   20
zoo   5, 9, 11, 19, 20, 22
zookeeping   5, 22
zoo kitchen   14